Apart from
Concrete Existence

poems by
Josef Krebs

More books available from:

Etched Press
www.etchedpress.com

Also available in Amazon Kindle Store

First edition
Cover art "Ghost in the Chimney"
Book design by Kevin Dublin

Dedicated to Ma Jeanne

Acknowledgments

The author wishes to acknowledge the editors of the following publications in which a few of these poems first appeared in earlier forms:

Agenda "You can still smell the chimneys"

Bicycle Review "Not Everything"

Calliope "Apart From Concrete Existence"

Corner Club Press "Ghosts Last Night"

FictionWeek Literary Review "I am savagely sad"

Mouse Tales Press "Unlikely Today"

CONTENTS

Not everything

Not everything

Is

About

And what is

About

Is unlikely

To be

About

You

Ghosts last night

Dreaming of the trinity
Father, son, and death
Death is the go-between
Passing from father to son
From son back to memories of father
Which father rejects like all life
In his pursuit of death
He escaped the camps
But he never escaped life
Which dragged him back behind the barbed wire
By his actions and choices
Until he became one with the chimney

I am savagely sad

I am savagely sad
And don't have a destination
But logic tries to guide
Me
Where illustrious fellowship
Of the subconscious
Would prove most fabulous
And uncanny while tremendous
Trepidation of creation
Through the plotting, plodding
Consciousness
Will leave me low and damp
Crystallizing all in innocuous
Random traipsing
Unchallenged or challenged
By the soldiers of the mind
Who come knocking mid-
Sentence
Arrest, try, and
Sentence
For ideas un-
Relenting
Yet
Unrestrained
Un-
Involved in creation

Apart from Concrete Existence

Tandemly traipsing
I sing the person
While she pedals
The petals of her cheeks
Drawn on canvas tablets
Beneath a spray of color
Organized into perfect
Balance of arrangement
Including seemingly random
Thoughts illuminating the power
Of the controlled chaos
Of interacting lines
Called lips

You can still smell the chimneys

You can still smell the chimneys
Amongst heavy ginger-breaded houses
And the sausages in mountains
Arch while the architecture changes
As you're crossing over the river
And they say the "work makes you free"
And a heaviness descends
While the stubborn autobahn stretches

Credibility
And the tanks are rolling in your mind
And the gypsy guitar player
You're traveling with is oblivious
Concerned more with lacquer on ghost nails
To build countless layers of history
That will protect the claws
That allow him to play
The cruel music that saddens all
While lifting the soul
To join countless other souls
In the ashes floating above
To be breathed in by all descendants
And traveling strangers

Unlikely Today

Today is not

Tomorrow

And certainly

Not

Yesterday

Today

Has no time

For yesterday

As tomorrow

Has no connection

To today

Tomorrow

Will find

Itself

In the past

Soon

Enough

After

Today has given

Way

To yesterday

So for now

Enjoy

The sun

Set slowly

Radar will detect your heart's sadness

Radar will detect your heart's sadness

While bombers fly overhead ready

To drop

You down

Causing death and destruction

Of the spirit

Tumbling buildings

A city in collapse

Bodies in strewn streets

Body collapses

In straw memories

Failure

Of memory

Too much

Too little

Each leeches

Lost in doubt

And dreams that disconcert

Raising more questions

Than you'll ever be able

To attempt to tackle

While lost children run

Amok saving their screams

For later dates

When their might might

Serve some purpose

Of creation

Technology has supersized life's lightness

Technology has supersized life's lightness
Replacing substance with fatness of empty experience
Meaning with quantity
Beauty with bounty
What will evolve?
What hope can be summoned
Whilst triviality rules and trepidation
Runs rampant
Casting aspersions on progress
Of the human
Soul heart mind
Better keep your doors locked

I realized that I have a photographic memory but I forgot to load the film

I realized that I have a photographic memory
but I forgot to load the film
So when nothing registers
Nothing happens
That you didn't want to
Tired or tied
Flooded or floundering
Eyesight refocused to see less of everyone
Though 2020 rules supreme
If you live that long
Faults and features dispersed
In seas of sadness and dissociation
With life lost on certain days
Or times
Until sight and memory reconcile
With circumstances and surroundings
So just remember to close the gate

Faster and frequently faster

Faster and frequently faster
I plaster my subconscious with posters
Demanding attention
Where the populace is unconcerned
And rivets mark the marred
Unchaperoned consequences
Like a bucket of lead bolts
Casting down the coastal highway
Drinking in unsolicited
Panache and courtly love
When what is called for is war and warriors
Dedicated to long lost foolish acquisitions
Lauded by simple many
Obstructed by anonymous few
While breath lasts
And cauldrons keep bubbling
Like tourist trinkets
And nobody cares
And nobody cares
And riches roll downhill to where
The rich are waiting
With laws and circumstance
Until we all rock back
And cringe
Hoping
Waiting for the ace to fall
And history gets discombobulated
Dripping down the side
Wasted
Unnecessary

For those that would
Will will
Convincing peasants that their power matters
Presides over all order
Until dynastic certitude is proved
Or convinces
Random people that random presence and power
Is ordained
Has worth and some claim
While death rushes up
Leaving all scattered
Soaked in necessary death and reality
That will some day free all idiots
Like me

And so, unchaperoned, I continue

And so, unchaperoned, I continue
Tantalizing the world with seductions chosen
From lost heritage chalices and trunks
Offering swarms of blessings and curses
To the world when it wanted
Waiting destruction where desired
And favored by first sons
And long lamented prodigals
Riding on rams
Down hill green and welcoming
While jealous brothers
Who'd played the game
To ingratiate with moneybags
Sacrificed life for expected reward
Left fallow dry and high
Like existence interrupted by love
Filial and favorite
Whilst mother marches off with her sheep
And nothing slows long enough
To make any experience worth while
Until the feast
Capsizes
Into miracles
That allow for hope
And purification
Until the morning

Soliciting answers to dreams unsought

Soliciting answers to dreams unsought
I drive myself down beneath the dirt
Like a corpse seeking solitude
When rapture can no longer be found
Amongst the butterflies
And treetops dampened by enigma
Rarely receive anything they might hope
To quell or question with insight
What they grow for
Taller than they'd ever known
Or desired
While leaves drop away
Into the past
As if energy transformation
Were a purpose
That made it all worth
While birds chirped encouragingly
Cheerleaders of optimism
Keeping horror at bay
Until the dogs track me down

Fevered, I now lash out at clinging hands

Fevered, I now lash out at clinging hands
Enwrapping perhaps
Or tenderly touching much concerned with what might
Or might not prevail
While I
Awake
Live in dreams
Riven by despair at circumstances
Believed as if intoxicant
Were coursing through blood and brain
Soliciting beliefs
Eliciting reactions
The speaking photographs
Conversing across space
Between frames
Of rational reference
Discussing me
With moving lips and nodding heads
Not startling my calm
As I observe
Just sparking curiosity
As sleeplessness burrowed
At minds and don't minds
Leaving reality in disarray
Until amnesia can get a grip

Uncomplicated uncompressed

Uncomplicated uncompressed
I dither on others' thoughts
Whist smart folks show me up
And show me down
To paths previously unfamiliar
Unsought or solicited
When harassment is all that's expected
But Beauty lies in wait when you least expect it
Gasoline drenching you in a moment
Of expectation
Of sudden resolutions
Trained on on by wild men
And wilderness
So that nothing is left
Beyond happiness
Carrion for life's fulfillment
When all has been promised
To evolution
As best you can

Rafters rift

Rafters rift, floors split and splinter

All is lost all is found

Naught caught but rhapsody

trapped

On occasion like a trout

Upstream dancing on its last line

Inclined to escape

But food for thought

Sadness scrambles

Sadness scrambles to try to keep up
Like a lost puppy on the moors
Barking in attempts to find its way home
To my heart
I'd probably be heartbroken
Without the sheath of the sad effervescence
Crawling over
Being
Like a lamb who serves her purpose
But was born for things other than slaughter
A life
To live
On planet Earth
Alongside humans
Who consider themselves
Too often
And other beings
Too little

I dove into a dive

I dove into a dive

On Washington

I had been sleepwalking

Through today

Like a bird in flight

Back from Africa

Asleep on the wing

When suddenly a cosh swung

And clipped me the edge

Skull beneath ear

I not quite divining avoiding

Through instinctual duck and dive

But keeping to feet

Staggering aside

Not felled just stunned

Whilst follow-up prepared cosh swung

'Til I slipped beneath swing

And came up on soft gut

And softer vulnerabilties

Upper cut cut

Large lad went down

In a spoiled dispersal

Of energy aimed

At disposal of own

Proposed venture

Into aforementioned

Divined dive

But a job's a ...

Soul killer crushing any wish

To survive

So

The lithe linger

The lithe linger
But the rest of us
Plant our feet enough
To be able to walk
And shrug off suggested occupations
Sleep to awake still to dreams
That cost but can carry us
Where we need where we were meant
To travel
Life lingers despite disappointment
The only thing you cared about
That kept you alive
The rest is survival
Which is necessary sometimes in history
To carry you through the days
You happen to exist in
While nothing goes on around you
Since it's only your experiences that matter